Historic Catholic Churches Along the Rio Grande in New Mexico

Historic Catholic Churches
Along the Rio Grande in New Mexico

David Policansky

SUNSTONE
PRESS

SANTA FE

On the front cover: San Miguel de Socorro Catholic Church, Socorro

On the back cover: San Antonio de Los Lentes Catholic Church, Los Lunas

Sunstone books may be purchased for educational, business, or sales promotional use.
For information please write: Special Markets Department, Sunstone Press,
P.O. Box 2321, Santa Fe, New Mexico 87504-2321.

Design › R. Ahl
Printed on acid-free paper
∞

———————————————

Library of Congress Cataloging-in-Publication Data

Names: Policansky, David, 1944- author.
Title: Historic Catholic churches along the Rio Grande in New Mexico /
    David Policansky.
Description: Santa Fe, NM : Sunstone Press, [2021] | Summary: "A
    photographic collection of New Mexico's historic Catholic churches along
    the Rio Grande"-- Provided by publisher.
Identifiers: LCCN 2021050034 | ISBN 9781632933645 (paperback) | ISBN
    9781632933683 (epub) | ISBN 1632933640 (paperback)
Subjects: LCSH: Catholic church buildings--New Mexico--Pictorial works. |
    Catholic church buildings--Rio Grande Region (Colo.-Mexico and
    Tex.)--Pictorial works. | LCGFT: Photobooks.
Classification: LCC NA4828 .P63 2021 | DDC
    246/.958209789--dc23/eng/20211028
LC record available at https://lccn.loc.gov/2021050034

———————————————

WWW.SUNSTONEPRESS.COM
SUNSTONE PRESS / POST OFFICE BOX 2321 / SANTA FE, NM 87504-2321 /USA
(505) 988-4418

Dedication

I dedicate this book to all the individuals and communities who care for and cherish their historic churches. Long may they and their churches endure.

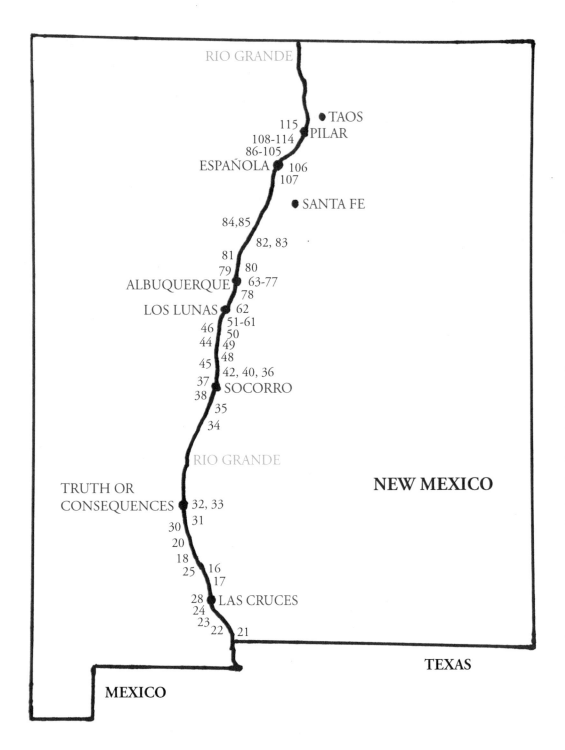

RIO GRANDE

● TAOS
115
108-114 PILAR
86-105
ESPAÑOLA ● 106
107

● SANTA FE

84,85
82, 83
81
79 80
ALBUQUERQUE ● 63-77
78
LOS LUNAS ● 62
46 51-61
50
44 49
48
45
42, 40, 36
37
38 SOCORRO
35
34

RIO GRANDE

NEW MEXICO

TRUTH OR
CONSEQUENCES ● 32, 33
31
30
20
18 16
25 17
28 LAS CRUCES
24
23 22 21

TEXAS

MEXICO

Approximate locations of the churches in this book. The numbers are the page numbers on which each church is illustrated and briefly described, and location information is given. In some areas, especially near Albuquerque and Española, there are too many churches to show each one individually on the map. This map, along with the directions to each individual church and a good highway atlas, should help in planning road trips to see groups of churches.

CONTENTS

INTRODUCTION

Catholic churches are an enormous part of New Mexico's history, culture, and landscapes. European settlement of New Mexico occurred earlier than in any other current U.S. state except Florida, when Juan de Oñate y Salazar settled near Española in 1598. The Franciscans who accompanied him brought Catholicism with them, and New Mexico was changed forever. The history of Spanish/Mexican rule and later U.S. rule in New Mexico, and the relationship of the Catholic Church to the indigenous peoples, is long, complicated, and sometimes ugly. That culture and history and how they interacted with those of the indigenous peoples then and now, influenced the types of Catholic churches in New Mexico and where they are today, and explains why churches of other Christian denominations weren't established in New Mexico until the 1850s, after it became a U.S. territory. The beauty of many old Catholic churches and of their locations is reward enough for exploring New Mexico, and it's a fine excuse for planning road trips. But appreciating their historical and cultural importance and how Catholicism interacted with New Mexico's indigenous peoples adds another dimension to that exploration, and to my motivation in creating this book. Some of the selected further readings (below) provide detailed discussions of these matters.

I have photographed all of the old Catholic churches I could find and access for this work. I have included all churches whose construction began by 1950, although also included are a few more-recent churches with historical value, design, or other appealing features. Photographs of a few interiors also are included. To my knowledge, no other book includes churches in New Mexico's southernmost counties as well as the north.

Although there are old Catholic churches in all parts of New Mexico, and I have tried to photograph all of them, this book focuses on the Rio Grande. The great river roughly divides New Mexico down its middle, and it was a critically important route for settlers and traders. For this book I have included churches from the Texas-New Mexico border to Pilar in Taos County, the south end of the steep Rio Grande Gorge. Upstream from there the river's gorge is too steep to support settlements and churches. The churches are grouped in the nine counties along the river, from south to north. For this book, I consider all churches visible from the river or its bosque (floodplain woods) as being in the Rio Grande region. Thus all churches in Albuquerque, Las Cruces, Bernalillo, and Socorro, for example, are in the Rio Grande region, but Santa Fe's churches are not.

Construction dates are a challenge. I have tried to find construction dates for each church illustrated here but in some cases, I could not.

In other cases, different sources gave different dates; in those cases, I used the date that seemed best documented. Whenever a sign at a church gives its construction date, I used that date. Similarly, where there was a sign outside a church, I usually used that version of the church's name, including the spelling. Do note that a sign giving the date of *establishment* of a church does not necessarily give its construction date, because many parishes or missions were established before the current church was built. Finally, some construction dates might have limited value in the face of extensive renovations and rebuilding of a church.

The photographs themselves are dated in case they might have historical value. I have given the location of every church with enough detail that with reasonable effort any of them can be found, recognizing that things, including roads and highway numbers, change over time. Sometimes, churches disappear, which added urgency to this project.

Making this book has deepened my appreciation of New Mexico's marvelous cultural and natural landscapes, including the fact that the descendants of these New Spanish/Mexican colonists have been here at least as long, and are just as American, as the descendants of the Mayflower pilgrims. Of course the indigenous peoples of America have been here much longer. I hope the book deepens your appreciation as well.

—Mountainair, New Mexico, 2021.

FINDING AND PHOTOGRAPHING NEW MEXICO'S CHURCHES

New Mexico has great richness and diversity in its Catholic churches, although none has the opulence of those in Europe and in Latin America. Many of New Mexico's older Catholic churches are along and near major waterways. In addition to the Rio Grande, the Chama, Mimbres, Mora, Pecos, Santa Cruz, and other rivers and their tributaries have many wonderful churches along and near them. Even some churches that are reached by dirt roads through rugged terrain turn out to be near streams. Most streams do not have roads alongside much of their distance, and so other than the Rio Grande and parts of the Pecos and Mimbres rivers, planning to drive along them is not an effective way to find churches. But there are other methods, which work for Rio Grande churches as well. Some of the books cited in the reading list are quite helpful in finding churches, as are websites, pamphlets, friends, and acquaintances. If you know someone who has lived in an area for a while, ask about churches. Then there is old-fashioned exploration. Do you see a place name on a map at the end of a road, or a road that passes through interesting areas? Go there. Be careful that you and your vehicle can handle the roads and the conditions, but much of the time you will be rewarded, if not by a gem of a church, by wonderful scenery. And there still will be detective work after you find the church; sometimes its name and often its construction date are not easy to find. Finally, please be respectful of private property and of local communities and their inhabitants. In my experience, people in small communities are proud of their churches and will gladly show them to you and tell you what they know about them, sometimes even unlocking gates for you. Many small rural churches are in need of funds for maintenance and restoration, and so I urge you to donate to them if given an opportunity. And be prepared to meet many dogs, which seem to abound around old rural churches.

Be especially careful in pueblos. Some allow photography of buildings, some require permits to take photographs, and others prohibit photography entirely.

Photographing older churches is a delightful challenge. For this book, I have tried to represent each church by a single photograph of the exterior with an interior photograph in some cases. This meant omitting various interesting or pleasing aspects of many churches, but my aim here has been to present the church in its best aspect while also providing an illustration that helps you identify the church, so I have tried to include the front of the church in each photograph.

In general, a church looks best when the light is on the front. Some churches face south, and they are a photographer's dream, because they have good light most of the day. But more churches face east than other directions, and a few even face north, which means they seldom have good light. I have been lucky that some remote churches that required difficult travel over rough terrain were bathed in glorious light on my first visit. In other cases, I have visited churches two and even three times to get good light, but in some cases I have had to accept light that was not optimal.

Another challenge can be presented by a church's surroundings, which might prevent one from getting to the best place for a photograph. These obstacles can include fences, telephone poles, other buildings, automobiles, ditches, private property, and other items. You do the best you can.

For those interested in technical details, my main camera is a 20.2 megapixel Canon 6D with a Canon EF 24-105 mm f/3.5-5.6 IS STM lens. This provides wide-angle to medium telephoto views. For harder-to-reach, more-distant churches, I use a Canon 100-400 mm f/4.5-5.6L IS II lens.

Organizations that Help Preserve and Restore Old Churches

Many individuals and organizations are interested in preserving New Mexico's history culture, and architecture, including its old Catholic churches, but not much money is available in many cases. Preserving old churches often depends on community and family efforts. Many churches have a *mayordomo* or *mayordoma*, individuals who take responsibility for taking care of and maintaining the church. Historically, these people were elected from the congregation or community each year, but today many of them maintain the role for years, even decades. They sometimes can help organizing fundraising and restoration efforts. Many small churches have collection boxes and the money collected often is used, at least in part, for maintenance and repair. Some more-formal organizations are listed below, and if they are not directly involved in funding or aiding preservation efforts, they often know who is. Websites are current at the time of publication of this book.

Archdiocese of Santa Fe Office of Historic Patrimony and Archives, www.archdiosf.org/archives

Cornerstones Community Partnerships, www.cstones.org

Historic Santa Fe Foundation, www.historicsantafe.org

New Mexico Historic Preservation Division, www.nmhistoricpreservation.org.

Nuevo Mexico Profundo, www.neuvo-mexico-profundo.org

Acknowledgments

Too many people to count have helped and encouraged me in this endeavor. I am grateful for all the publications on New Mexico's churches that precede this one, and I have used information in them. Of those authors, the Archdiocese of Santa Fe, in particular Bernadette Lucero in the Office of Artistic-Historic Patrimony and Archives; Marie Romero Cash; Frank Graziano; and John Taylor have provided information and encouragement. Marie Cash also provided valuable editorial suggestions and factual corrections. Donna Vargas, historian of the Diocese of Las Cruces; Gretchen Brock, historian with the New Mexico Historic Preservation Division; and Christian Mericle of Tucumcari also have been helpful with information on individual churches, and Carlos Trujillo gave me an extensive tour of the Santa Cruz de Cañada Church and its fabulous art. Kerri Hallihan reviewed some of the text for me with helpful suggestions. Many people at parishes I have contacted have been kind and generous with information.

I also am grateful to the many individuals I have met in my travels who have generously shown me and told me about their churches, and pointed me toward others I was not aware of. Their kindness and pride in their churches have been an inspiration.

Finally, my wife, Sheila David, has been a partner on many of my "churching expeditions," as we call them, usually a willing and patient partner. She has pointed out features of the churches that I might have missed otherwise and suggested ways for me to take better photographs, and helped me choose among the photographs I have taken. When my planned trips were too extensive for any normal person to enjoy, she encouraged me to have fun and find good churches. I am more than grateful for those gifts from her.

Churches by County

Our Lady of Purification Catholic Church, Doña Ana (Doña Ana County). 1865. The modern church is next door to this lovely old one, which was being restored when I took this photograph in 2019. At 5525 Cristo Rey Street.

Our Lady of Health Catholic Church, Las Cruces (Doña Ana County). 1998. This recent church is included because it is large and striking. The architect was Lorenzo Aguilar. At 1178 North Mesquite Street. Photograph taken in 2019.

Our Lady of All Nations Mission Catholic Church, Rincon (Doña Ana County). 1919. Extensively renovated within the past 15 years. The statue is of Our Lady of Šiluva of Lithuania. At 1993 Rincon Road. Photograph taken in 2021.

Our Lady of Guadalupe Shrine and Parish Catholic Church, Tortugas (just southeast of Mesilla Park in Doña Ana County). 1913. This unusual-looking church is at 3600 Paroquia Street. Photograph taken in 2021.

St. Francis de Sales Catholic Church, Rodey (Doña Ana County). 1860. The church was sold to private owners in 1963 and has been sold several times since then. On Florencio Lopez Street. Photograph taken in 2019.

San Martín de Porres Catholic Church, Sunland Park (Doña Ana County). 1991. At 1885 McNutt Road, this striking church is near the Texas border. Martín de Porres (1579–1639), a Peruvian of mixed race, is the patron saint for racial harmony. Photograph taken in 2019.

San Luis Rey Catholic Church, Chamberino (Doña Ana County). About 1900. The church was built on higher ground after floods ruined homes and an earlier church. At 334 San Luis Avenue. Photograph taken in 2019.

San José Catholic Church, La Mesa (Doña Ana County). 1860. At 353 Josephine Street. This state historical monument has received some repairs since this photograph was taken in 2019.

San Miguel Catholic Church, San Miguel (Doña Ana County). Late 1800s. This striking church is built from local lava rock, which is not a common construction material. On New Mexico Highway 28. Photograph taken in 2019

La Capilla de Don Silverio, near Hatch (Doña Ana County). Probably after 1950. This remote chapel perched on a steep rise is down Arroyo Cuervo Road and then two miles farther down an unnamed dirt road near the Rio Grande. The photo of the interior was taken through the door. The prominently displayed images of Santo Niño de Atocha suggest that the chapel might be named for him. Photographs taken in 2020.

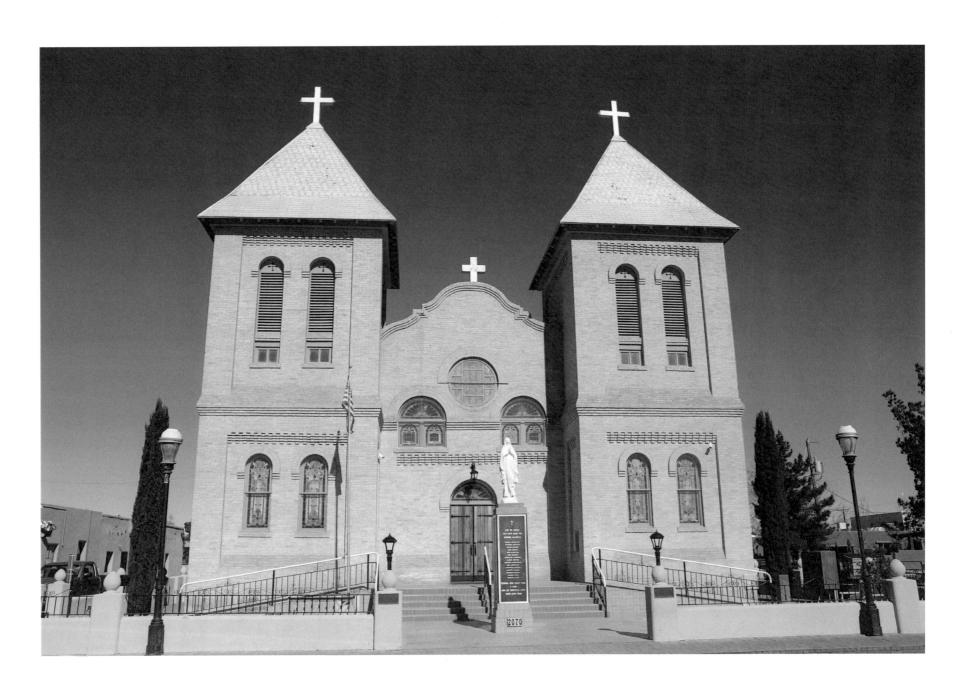

Catholic Basilica de San Albino, Mesilla (Doña Ana County). 1906. A lovely, cathedral-like church. On the plaza. Photograph taken in 2017.

Catholic Basilica de San Albino interior, Mesilla (Doña Ana County). 1906. The striking interior shows some of the statues, but not the altar and crucifix, draped in purple before Easter. Photograph taken in 2017.

San José Catholic Church, Arrey (Sierra County). 1891. It is fairly unusual for the main entrance to be on the side rather than in front of the building. On New Mexico Highway 187 south of Caballo Reservoir. Photograph taken in 2019.

San Isidro Catholic Church, Las Palomas (Sierra County). 1945. The church is fenced off but seemingly is in good repair. It was built to replace an earlier church inundated when Caballo Reservoir was filled. Exit 71 east off I-25. Photograph taken in 2020.

Our Lady of Perpetual Health Catholic Church, Truth or Consequences (Sierra County). Early 1920s. This original church building is now the parish hall, and the newer church (opposite) is across the parking lot. On North Date Street. Photograph taken in 2020.

The current Our Lady of Perpetual Health Catholic Church, Truth or Consequences (Sierra County). 1949. On North Date Street. The church, pale pink at midday, appears yellow near sunset in this photograph, taken in 2020

San Antonio Catholic Mission Church, San Antonio (Socorro County). 1930. The building has become unstable and since about 2017 has been fenced off. Attempts are being made to raise funds for restoration. On New Mexico Highway 1. Photograph taken in 2013.

San José Catholic Mission Church, Luis Lopez (Socorro County). About 1900. The exterior of this church has changed little, if at all, since it was built. On New Mexico Highway 1. Photograph taken in 2019.

San José Catholic Mission Church, San Acacia (Socorro County). Built in the 1940s and abandoned in 1957, it was still hanging on in this photograph taken in 2019. Exit 163 off I-25, head east.

San Antonio Catholic Mission Church, Alamillo (Socorro County). 1928. Close inspection shows a dove on the left, guano-stained steeple of this unusual church. San Acacia exit (163) off I-25; head west. Photograph taken in 2019.

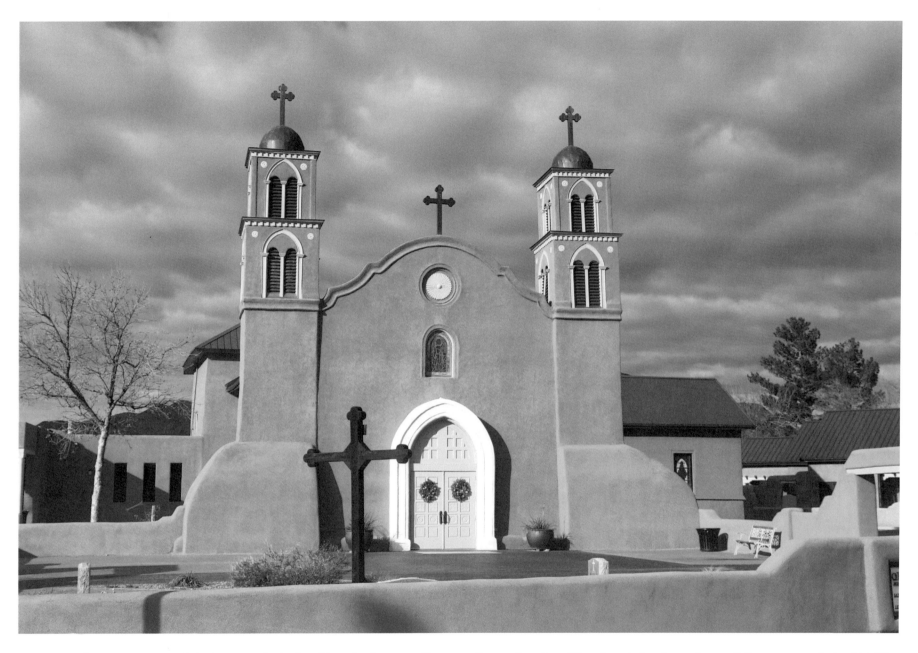

The magnificent San Miguel de Socorro Catholic Church, Socorro (Socorro County). 1821. The church has been beautifully renovated. At 403 El Camino Real. Photograph taken in 2019.

San Miguel de Socorro Catholic Church, interior; Socorro (Socorro County). 1821. Photograph taken in 2018.

La Sagrada Familia Catholic Church, Lemitar (Socorro County). 1830s, rebuilt in 2015 after a wall collapsed during restoration. Modeled after San Miguel in Socorro, its interior is modest but not spartan. Exit 156 off I-25; on New Mexico Highway 408. Photograph taken in 2018.

La Sagrada Familia Catholic Church interior, Lemitar (Socorro County). Photograph taken in 2018.

San Lorenzo Catholic Mission Church, Polvadera (Socorro County). 1925. Notice the separate bell in an elaborate adobe housing. Exit 163 off I-25 then south on the frontage road to Polvadera Road. Photograph taken in 2019.

San Isidro Catholic Mission Church, Las Nutrias (Socorro County). 1894 or earlier; different sources have different dates for this church, some as late as 1935. On New Mexico Highway 304. Photograph taken in 2014.

Cristo Rey Catholic Church, Bosque (Sabinal, Socorro County). 1929. The church bell is on its own detached metal support. On New Mexico Highway 116. Photograph taken in 2013.

Unidentified Catholic chapel in Veguita (Socorro County). A neighbor told me that the chapel was built privately in the 1800s. On New Mexico Highway 304. Photograph taken in 2019.

San Antonio de Padua Catholic Church, Abeytas (Socorro County). 1874, recently restored. This adobe church is quite traditional. On New Mexico Highway 116. Photograph taken in 2019.

San Antonio de Padua Catholic Church interior, Abeytas (Socorro County). Notice the hand-carved corbels (viga supports). Photograph taken in 2019.

Our Lady of Sorrows Catholic Church, La Joya (Socorro County). 1817–1830. In addition to the bell tower at the rear, there is another bell and cross on a detached metal support in front of the church. An earlier photograph shows this adobe church painted white. On Calle de la Iglesia. Photograph taken in 2020.

San José Catholic Mission Church, Contreras (Socorro County). 1906. The church has three crosses on the roof. On New Mexico Highway 304 around mile marker 3 on the west side of the highway. Photograph taken in 2019.

Immaculate Conception Catholic Church, Casa Colorada (Valencia County). 1949. The church, in a sparsely populated region, evokes great loneliness. The luminarias in this December 2014 photograph were not present in December 2018, possibly suggesting disuse. On New Mexico Highway 304.

San Antonio de Los Lentes Catholic Church, Los Lunas (Valencia County). Original build date 1789 with frequent modifications since then. The "triple tin hat" design is quite unusual. On Los Lentes Road NE. Photograph taken in 2014.

San Antonio Catholic Church, Bosque (Valencia County). 1936. The church bell is in a separate support on the right. There are three crosses on the roof. On New Mexico Highway 116. Photograph taken in 2013.

Nuestra Señora de la Immaculada Concepción Catholic Church, Tomé (Valencia County). 1746 (bell towers added in 2013). The oldest church in Valencia County. Off New Mexico Highway 47. Photograph taken in 2018.

Our Lady of Guadalupe Catholic Church, Los Chavez (Valencia County). 1857. In Our Lady of Sorrows Parish of Belen, this church has a simple, neo-Gothic design. On Guadalupe Road off New Mexico Highway 314. Photograph taken in 2019.

Sangre de Cristo Catholic Church, Valencia (Valencia County). 1942. The art above the doorway is painted on panels. On New Mexico Highway 47. Photograph taken in 2018.

Our Lady of Guadalupe Catholic Church, Peralta (Valencia County). About 1850. The unusual design of this adobe church, including the circular window, is striking. On New Mexico Highway 47. Photograph taken in 2008.

San Francisco Xavier Catholic Church, Jarales (Valencia County). 1976. The 1875 church on this site collapsed as restoration began in 1975; I include this newer church as an argument for honoring the spirit of the old when restoration is impossible. South on Jarales Road to Crawford Road off Reinken Avenue. Photograph taken in 2019.

Old store, Tomé (Valencia County), repurposed into a Penitente Brotherhood morada. Privately owned. On New Mexico Highway 47 in Tomé just north of mile marker 25, very close to the route of the annual Easter pilgrimage to Tomé Hill. Photograph taken in 2019.

San Clemente Parish Catholic Church, Los Lunas (Valencia County). 1949–1954, extensively renovated (or rebuilt) in 2002. On Luna Road NE. Photograph taken in 2021.

Chapel of Our Lady of Refuge, Belen (Valencia County). 1877. Rebuilt from a chapel built in 1850, it was moved to its present location in 1905. Now deconsecrated, it is a private residence. On Barboa Road at Don Felipe Road. Photograph taken in 2021.

Private chapel in Los Lunas (Valencia County). One of the more elaborate private chapels, beautifully maintained. On New Mexico Highway 47 north of MM 29. Photograph taken in 2021.

Saint Augustine (San Agustín) Mission Catholic Church, Isleta Pueblo (Bernalillo County). First built in 1613, it was burned in the Pueblo Revolt of 1680. Rebuilt on the remaining walls in 1716 and renovated since then, it is one of the oldest and finest mission churches in New Mexico. Photograph taken in 2020.

San Ignacio Catholic Church, Albuquerque (Bernalillo County). 1916. This church is less well known than San Felipe de Neri (following pages), but it nonetheless is quite striking, including the colorful statues. At 1300 Walter Street NE. Photograph taken in 2019.

San Felipe de Neri Catholic Church, Albuquerque (Bernalillo County). 1793. One of the more spectacular old churches in New Mexico. On the Old Town plaza. Photograph taken in 2019.

San Felipe de Neri Catholic Church interior, Albuquerque (Bernalillo County). 1793. The church is usually open to visitors. Photograph taken in 2019.

Los Duranos Catholic Chapel, Albuquerque (Bernalillo County). 1890. Now a private residence, it has been preserved externally. The two junipers largely hide its front aspect. At 2601 Indian School Road NW. Photograph taken in 2019.

Santa Cruz Capía de Los Tomases, Albuquerque (Bernalillo County). Early 1920s. The building in the background was not present in a 1984 photo of this chapel. At 3101 Los Tomases Drive NW. Photograph taken in 2020.

Our Lady of Mount Carmel, Albuquerque (Bernalillo County), 1870. This handsome adobe church is tucked away at 7805 Edith Boulevard. NE, in Los Ranchos de Albuquerque not far from the Rio Grande. Photograph taken in 2019.

Los Candelarias or San Antonio Catholic Chapel, Albuquerque (Bernalillo County). 1888. Deconsecrated in the 1950s, the chapel is now a private residence. At 1934 Candelaria Road NW. Photograph taken in 2020.

Nativity of the Blessed Virgin Mary Catholic Church, Alameda (Bernalillo County). 1911. This large, handsome church replaced earlier ones in the area and is on the site of a former Tewa pueblo. At 9502 4th Street NW. Photograph taken in 2019.

Catholic Chapel of Our Lady of Guadalupe, Albuquerque (Bernalillo County). 1890. At 1860 Griegos Road NW, it is near a larger modern church. Photograph taken in 2019.

Old San José Catholic Church, Albuquerque (Bernalillo County). 1925. Across the parking lot from the newer church (opposite), the church has elements of California Mission and Pueblo Revival styles. At 2401 Broadway Boulevard SE. Photograph taken in 2019.

The new San José Parish Church, Albuquerque (Bernalillo County), across the parking lot from the old one. 2008. This church is very large. At 2401 Broadway Boulevard SE. Photograph taken in 2019.

San Francisco Xavier Catholic Church, Albuquerque (Bernalillo County). 1949. This handsome church is mainly in the Pueblo Revival style. At 820 Broadway Boulevard SE. Photograph taken in 2019.

Saint Joseph on the Rio Grande Catholic Church, Albuquerque (Bernalillo County). Early 2000s. I included this church because of the rendering of traditional design with a modern touch. At 5901 St. Joseph's Drive NW. Photograph taken in 2019.

Santo Niño Catholic Church, Carnuel (Bernalillo County). 1960. This old-style church replaced one built in the 1890s. Easy to see from I-40, it is not so easy to find. Take the Carnuel exit to 5 Herrera Road SE. Photograph taken in 2019.

Saint Charles Borromeo Catholic Church, Albuquerque (Bernalillo County). 1934. Carlo Borromeo was archbishop of Milan in the 16th century and was a member of a very powerful, wealthy family. At 1818 Coal Place SE. Photograph taken in 2021.

San Isidro, Pajarito (Bernalillo County). Mid-1800s or earlier. Formerly a Catholic church, this building now is a county visitor center. The art by Esteban Duran (1997) on the former door is titled "The Settler." At 6080 Isleta Boulevard SW. Photograph taken in 2021.

San Ysidro Catholic Church, Corrales (Sandoval County). Built in 1868, the church was deconsecrated 1962 when a new church (not pictured) was completed. It is maintained and used for secular events. On Church Road. Photograph taken in 2019.

Santuario de San Lorenzo (Catholic Shrine of St. Lawrence), Bernalillo (Sandoval County). About 1857. The newer Our Lady of Sorrows Catholic Church is next to this shrine. At 281 Camino del Pueblo. Photograph taken in 2019.

San José Mission Catholic Church, Algodones (Sandoval County). 1900. This unusual church is at 1415 New Mexico Highway 313. Photograph taken in 2019.

San Antonio de Padua Catholic Church, Sandia Pueblo (Sandoval County). 1864. The church building has been condemned and it is no longer in use. Photograph taken from New Mexico Highway 313 in 2019.

New San Antonio de Padua Catholic Church, Sandia Pueblo (Sandoval County). Around 2002. This large, Pueblo-Revival-style church replaced the one opposite. Photograph taken from New Mexico Highway 313 in 2019.

Santa Bárbara Catholic Mission Church, Sile (Sandoval County). A neighbor told me that the church was built before 1900 and is still used. On Sile Road between Cochiti and Santo Domingo pueblos, currently accessible only through the latter. Photograph taken in 2021.

Morada of the Penitente Brotherhood, Peña Blanca (Sandoval County). This morada looks more like a church than most do, and unusually has an identifying sign. Probably before 1900. On New Mexico Highway 22. Photograph taken in 2021.

La Capilla de Sangre de Cristo, Cuarteles (Quarteles on most maps; Santa Fe County). 1849. This attractive church is on New Mexico Highway 76 near Española. Photograph taken in 2021.

La Capilla del Santo Niño de Atocha, Santa Cruz (Santa Fe County). 1934. On New Mexico Highway 76. Photograph taken in 2019.

La Capilla de Nacimiento de Niño Dios, La Puebla (Santa Fe County). 1876. Funds and a restoration plan are in place for this church, which has sadly deteriorated in recent years. On La Placita Road off New Mexico Highway 76. Photograph taken in 2021.

La Capilla de la Sagrada Familia, Pajarito (Santa Fe County). Early 1920s, restored in the 1990s. Surrounded by San Ildefonso Pueblo. This photograph was taken in 2020 from New Mexico Highway 30; the sacred Black Mesa is just out of the frame to the right.

San Antonio de Padua Mission Catholic Church, El Rancho (Santa Fe County). 1938. This striking church has a California feel to it. On County Road 84 just east of San Ildefonso Pueblo. Photograph taken in 2021.

La Capilla de Nuestra Señora del Carmen, Santa Cruz (Santa Fe County). 1940s. This chapel is about two blocks north of Santa Cruz de Cañada Church on the following pages. Photograph taken in 2021.

Santa Cruz de Cañada Catholic Church, Santa Cruz (Santa Fe County). 1733. This beautiful church is one of the oldest in New Mexico, and unusually it has changed relatively little since it was built. At 116 S. McCurdy Road. Photograph taken in 2020.

The interior of Santa Cruz Catholic Church, opposite. This grand church is filled with glorious art, including pieces by famed santero Rafael Aragon (1795–1862). Photograph taken in 2021.

San José de Chama Catholic Church, Hernández (Rio Arriba County). 1850. This church is in Ansel Adams's famous photograph Moonrise, Hernandez. It now is used as a morada by the Penitente Brotherhood. On County Road 0001. Photograph taken in 2019.

San Francisco de Asís Catholic Mission Church, El Duende (Rio Arriba County). Hard to find, this church is off Roybal Road off New Mexico Highway 74 near US Highway 84/285, on private property. Photograph taken in 2021.

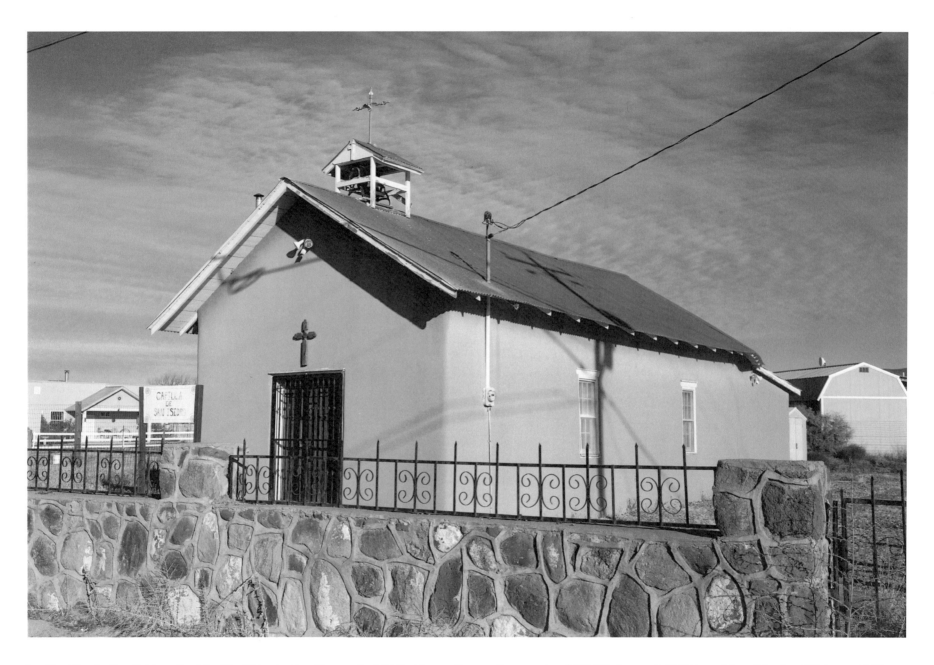

La Capilla de San Isidro, La Mesilla (Rio Arriba County). 1918. About three miles south of US Highway 84/285 on New Mexico Highway 399, this chapel is still in use. Photograph taken in 2021.

La Capilla de San Pedro, Española (Rio Arriba Co.). About 1900. The gate has an image of Saint Peter (San Pedro) holding a key. On Lower San Pedro Road. Photograph taken in 2021.

San Raphael de El Guique (Rio Arriba County). 1900. The recently added large portico is disproportionate and detracts from the otherwise pleasing architecture of the church. Off County Road 58 near the large cemetery of the same name. Photograph taken in 2021.

La Capilla de San Pedro, Okay Owingeh Pueblo in Chamita (Rio Arriba County). 1875. There is a large camposanto (cemetery) close by this church. On County Road 56. Photograph taken in 2020.

Nuestra Señora de Guadalupe Catholic Mission Church, Guachupangue (Rio Arriba County). Early 1800s. The armchair-like buttresses are unusual. On County Road 2 about 1/3 mile from its junction with New Mexico Highway 30. Photograph taken in 2021.

San Antonio de Padua Catholic Mission Church, El Guache (Rio Arriba County). 1900. The portico is a recent addition. Just off US Highway 84/285, fronting on El Camino Abajo Road. Photograph taken in 2021.

Catholic Chapel of San Francisco de Asís, Estaca (Rio Arriba County). 1930. On New Mexico Highway 582 at mile-marker 4. Photograph taken in 2021.

La Capilla de San Miguel, Española (Rio Arriba County). 1820s. This chapel is surrounded by a fence with a locked gate. On Calle San Miguel off New Mexico Highway 68. Photograph taken in 2021.

Private chapel dedicated to Nuestra Señora de San Juan de los Lagos in Arroyo Seco near Española (Rio Arriba County), at La Puebla Road and US Highway 84/285. It was built in 2001–2010 by Luis Atencio (1925–2011), a local restaurateur. Photograph taken in 2019.

Sacred Heart of Jesus Catholic Parish Church, Española (Rio Arriba County). 1929, renovated 1947. At 908 W. Calle Rosario. Photograph taken in 2019.

San Juan Bautista Catholic Church, Okay Owingeh Pueblo (Rio Arriba County). 1913. This neo-Gothic brick building replaced an adobe church dating to 1706. In the center of the pueblo. Photograph taken in 2020.

Catholic Chapel of Our Lady of Lourdes, Ohkay Owingeh Pueblo (Rio Arriba County). 1890. Across the plaza from San Juan Bautista church opposite. The stone probably was from the quarry also used for the Loretto Chapel in Santa Fe. Photograph taken in 2020.

Saint Anne Catholic Church, Alcalde (Rio Arriba County). About 1964. Quite traditional despite being fairly recent. On New Mexico Highway 68. Photograph taken in 2019.

Old Saint Anne Catholic Church, Alcalde (Rio Arriba County). About 1900. This is behind the newer church opposite. Stone buttresses of this style are common in this part of northern New Mexico but not elsewhere. Photograph taken in 2019.

Our Lady of Guadalupe Chapel, Los Luceros Historic Site (Rio Arriba County). 1889. The chapel was deeded to the Archdiocese of Santa Fe in 1891. On County Road 41 between Alcalde and Velarde. Photograph taken in 2021.

Iglesia de la Virgen de Guadalupe (Our Lady of Guadalupe Catholic Church), Velarde (Rio Arriba County). 1817. This adobe church is just off County Road 41, with a sign on New Mexico Highway 68. Photograph taken in 2019.

San Antonio de Padua, Alcalde (Rio Arriba County). 1878, rebuilt 1954. This charming adobe church with its stone buttresses is in the old church plaza of Alcalde on County Road 41. Photograph taken in 2021.

Possibly Our Lady of Solitude, La Villita (Rio Arriba County). 1913. There is a painting of Our Lady of Guadalupe on the back of the chapel. On County Road 41 near its junction with County Road 42. Photograph taken in 2021.

San José Catholic Church, Lyden (Rio Arriba County). 1897. This unusually low-slung church has the stone buttresses of the style often seen in this region. New Mexico Highway 582 across the Rio Grande, then right on County Road 59 to number 28. Photograph taken in 2021.

Nuestra Señora de los Dolores Catholic Church, Pilar (Taos County). 1892. New Mexico Highway 570 off New Mexico Highway 68. Upstream of here the river's gorge becomes very steep. Photograph taken in 2019.

Selected Further Readings

Archdiocese of Santa Fe. 1998. *Four Hundred Years of Faith: Seeds of Struggle, Harvest of Faith*. An information-filled history of the Catholic Church in New Mexico with information about every parish in the archdiocese and photographs of each parish church. Some additional information on the missions of parishes is also given.

Brewer, Robert, and Steve McDowell. 1990. *The Persistence of Memory: New Mexico's Churches*. Museum of New Mexico Press. A historical approach with idiosyncratically chosen photographic illustrations.

Cash, Marie Romero. 1993. *Built of Earth and Song: Churches of Northern New Mexico. A Guide*. Red Crane Books. With monocrhome photographs and maps. Cash is a noted santera (painter of images of saints), and her book is a favorite of mine. Church locations are given, but a few have little detail.

Dakin, William. 2013. *Rural Churches of Northern New Mexico: A Personal Selection*. Beech River Books. A charming book of Dakin's paintings of churches, with directions to them. This book has some errors in church identifications and of construction details, but it is delightful and helped me considerably.

Gibson, Daniel. 2011. *Pueblos of the Rio Grande: A Visitor's Guide*. Rio Nuevo Publishers. Most pueblos have historic churches and Gibson's book is a useful guide to when and how to see them and whether photography is allowed in the pueblos.

Graziano, Frank. 2019. *Historic Churches of New Mexico Today*. Oxford University Press. An in-depth look at the history of Catholicism and Catholic churches in New Mexico with an emphasis on current conditions. This excellent book has few illustrations of churches but provides detailed directions to quite a few of them.

Julyan, Robert. 1998. *The Place Names of New Mexico, 2nd Edition*. University of New Mexico Press. An indispensable guide, written with humor, insight, and great erudition.

Kessell, John. 2012. *The Missions of New Mexico since 1776*. Sunstone Press. An update of Fray Francisco Atanasio Dominguez's inventory The Missions of New Mexico, 1776, this book covers the surviving mission churches, including several in this book.

Lux, Annie, and Daniel Nadelbach. 2007. *Historic New Mexico Churches*. Gibbs Smith Press. A selection of New Mexico's most historic churches graced with Nadelbach's glorious color photographs.

Nava, Margaret. 2004. *Along the High Road: A Guide to the Scenic Route Between Española and Taos*. Sunstone Press. Despite its being 16 years old, this still is a useful guide to the history, art, and culture of the region, including information about lodging and restaurants, and it has information about several historic Catholic churches. With monochrome photographs.

Nava, Margaret. 2006. *Remembering, A Guide to New Mexico Cemeteries, Monuments and Memorials*. Sunstone Press. Describes some selected New Mexico cemeteries, including information on churches when they are adjacent to the cemeteries. With monochrome photographs.

Santa Cruz de la Cañada Parish. 2015. *La Iglesia de la Santa Cruz de la Cañada, 2nd Edition*. A detailed illustrated history of the church from 1695 to 2015 and the restoration of its fabulous art, with some information on other churches in the parish. Mostly in English but some Spanish.

Taylor, John. 2011. *Catholics along the Rio Grande*. Arcadia Publishing. An account of the spread of Catholics and their churches along New Mexico's great river, with many monochrome photographs, including historical ones. Taylor's definition of the Rio Grande region is based on parishes, some of which cover large areas, and hence is much broader than mine, including some churches in the East Mountain region as well as churches as far east as Picacho and as far west as Quemado. His book covers the region from Isleta south to Truth or Consequences and provides much information on construction dates of churches.

Wallis, Michael. 2018. Los *Luceros: New Mexico's Morning Star*. University of New Mexico Press. Lavishly illustrated with Gene Peach's photographs, the book is an extensive history of this region of the Rio Grande focused on what was originally a 51,000-acre land grant, and now is a New Mexico Historic Site of around 148 acres.

Glossary of Spanish Terms and Names

Adobe: Building material made from earth and organic material.

Agustín, Augustine: Saint Augustine of Hippo, North Africa, 354–430 AD.

Albino, Albinus: Saint Albinus of Angers, France, 470–550 AD.

Ana, Anne: Saint Anne was Mary's mother, Jesus's grandmother.

Antonio, Anthony: Saint Anthony of Padua, born in Lisbon 1195, died 1231 in Padua.

Arriba, Above, upper: The Rio Arriba is the upper Rio Grande, above about the middle of Sandoval County; the lower river, or Rio Abajo, extends south to about Belen.

Asís, Assisi: Town in Italy, home of Saint Francis.

Bárbara, Barbara, Saint Barbara: Lebanese and Greek saint and martyr, about 250–300 AD.

Bautista, Baptist: St. John the Baptist.

Camposanto: Cemetery.

Capía: Alternate spelling of capilla.

Capilla: Chapel.

Carmen, Carmel: Mount Carmel in the Holy Land, now Israel.

Clemente, Clement: Pope, 35–99 AD.

Concepción Immaculada: Immaculate Conception (the Catholic doctrine that Mary was conceived free of original sin).

Corbel: A structure, usually of wood, supporting the end of a beam.

Cristo: Christ.

Cruz (plural, cruces): Cross.

Dios: God.

Dolores: Sorrows.

Felipe, Philip, Filippo Neri: Italian priest, 1515–1595.

Francisco, Francis: Saint Francis of Assisi, died 1226; Saint Francis Xavier, Spanish Missionary, 1506–1552.

Grande: Great, large.

Ignacio, Ignatius: Saint Ignatius, Spanish priest, 1491–1556.

Isidro, Isidore: Usually Saint Isidore the Farmer (Labrador), Spanish farmworker, 1082–1172.

José, Joseph: Saint Joseph, Mary's husband, legal father of Jesus.

Juan, John: Saint John the Apostle or Saint John the Baptist.

Lorenzo, Lawrence: Saint Lawrence of Rome, deacon and martyr, 225–258 AD.

Luis Rey, Louis the King: Louis IX, king of France and saint, 1214–1270; canonized 1294.

Martín, Martin: San Martín de Porres, Peruvian, 1579–1639.

Morada: Meeting house for members of the Penitente Brotherhood.

Miguel, Michael: Archangel Michael.

Nacimiento: Birth.

Niño: Child.

Nuestra Señora (de), Our Lady (of), The Virgin Mary: Usually followed by los Dolores (Sorrows), or other aspects of her life or community circumstances; or by a place name, such as Guadalupe in Mexico, where apparitions of the Virgin Mary occurred.

Parroquia: Parish church.

Pedro, Peter: Saint Peter, apostle and first Pope.

Rafael, Raphael: Archangel Raphael, first mentioned 3rd century BCE.

Rey: King.

Rio: River.

Sagrada: Sacred, holy.

Sagrada Familia: Holy Family.

San, Santa, Santo: Saint.

Santa, Santo: Holy.

Sangre: Blood.

Santera, Santero: A maker of carved or painted images of saints.

Viga: A beam in the ceiling of an adobe building, often supported by corbels. Exposed ends of vigas projecting beyond the exterior walls are typical of Pueblo and Spanish colonial architecture, and are in some famous adobe churches in New Mexico.

Virgen: Virgin.

Ysidro, Isidore: see Isidro.

Index

INDEX TO CHURCHES BY LOCATION

CPSIA information can be obtained
at www.ICGtesting.com
Printed in the USA
LVRC102145110222
710956LV00001B/5

9 781632 933645